FEMALE
SPORTS STARS

Superstars of Women's Basketball

Superstars of Women's Figure Skating

Superstars of Women's Golf

Superstars of Women's Gymnastics

Superstars of Women's Tennis

Superstars of Women's Track and Field

CHELSEA HOUSE PUBLISHERS

FEMALE SPORTS
STARS

SUPERSTARS OF WOMEN'S GYMNASTICS

Joel H. Cohen

CHELSEA HOUSE PUBLISHERS
Philadelphia

CHELSEA HOUSE PUBLISHERS

Produced by Daniel Bial Agency and Associates
New York, New York

Senior Designer   Cambraia Magalhães
Picture Research   Sandy Jones
Cover Illustration   Neil Maclachlan
Frontispiece   A multiple-exposure photo of Nadia Comaneci performing a flip on the balance beam at the 1976 Olympics. *[AP]*

3 5 7 9 8 6 4 2

Library of Congress Cataloging-in-Publication Data

Cohen, Joel H.
        Superstars of women's gymnastics / Joel H. Cohen
        p. cm. — (Female sports stars)
        Includes bibliographical references (p.) and index.
        Summary: Discusses the evolution of gymnastic competition and the role of women in the sport, highlighting the careers of Olga Korbut, Nadia Comaneci, Mary Lou Retton, and Shannon Miller.
        ISBN 0-7910-4391-6 (hardcover)
        1. Women gymnasts—Biography—Juvenile literature. 2. Gymnastics for women—History—Juvenile literature. [1. Gymnasts. 2. Gymnastics. 3. Women—Biography.] I. Title. II. Series.
GV460.C65 1996
796.44'092'2—dc20
[B]   96-321555
                                                                                              CIP
                                                                                               AC

CONTENTS

CHAPTER 1
AN EXPLOSION OF TALENT 7

CHAPTER 2
OLGA KORBUT:
A RUSSIAN REVOLUTION 13

CHAPTER 3
NADIA COMANECI:
FIRST IN PERFECTION 19

CHAPTER 4
MARY LOU RETTON:
ONE GREAT LEAP 29

CHAPTER 5
SHANNON MILLER:
MOST DECORATED AMERICAN 41

CHAPTER 6
TODAY'S STARS 49

CHRONOLOGY 62
SUGGESTIONS FOR
FURTHER READING 63
INDEX 64

1

AN EXPLOSION
OF TALENT

The instant the green light flashes, the graceful, slight, young woman races forward along a narrow, 82-foot-long runway, gathering speed as she goes. Without a moment's hesitation, she bounces off a springboard, seemingly exploding into the air. For less than a second, her feet well off the ground, she touches her hands onto a four-foot high, fourteen-inch-wide piece of gym apparatus called the "horse." She immediately pushes off, launching herself into a series of complex and difficult twists, turns, and flips, before landing firmly on the mat.

In this competition, known as the vault (one of four events in women's gymnastics), the athlete is judged on how high and far she traveled from the horse, as well as the number, quality, and difficulty of her twists or somersaults. The greater the degree of difficulty, the

Cathy Rigby was America's first great gymnast.

higher the score. The slightest hop or wobble on the landing can create a tenth of a point deduction—and can be the difference between winning a medal or not.

All the events call for the performer to demonstrate courage, strength, concentration, coordination, precision, and split-second timing. One of these events, the uneven bars, may be the most spectacular, as all forward and backward movements must flow uninterrupted from one to the next. One bar is about two feet higher than the other, creating opportunities for a variety of breathtaking moves: handstands, releases, pirouettes, and great circles all before a stylish dismount.

The balance beam is a wooden apparatus only four inches wide. As one writer put it, "The only thing that easy to do on it is fall off." Indeed, many gymnasts have done just that, while attempting to execute a series of harmoniously blended acrobatic and gymnastic movements as if they were performing on the floor, not a narrow strip off the ground.

In her 70- to 90-second routine, which must cover the beam's entire 16-foot length, the gymnast tumbles, leaps, turns, and may do a fiendishly difficult back salto—which requires the athlete to know where to land her feet without actually seeing the beam.

The fourth event calls for the athlete to demonstrate her personality and creativity, along with her athleticism, balance, and flexibility. The floor exercise provides nothing but a 40-foot-square area on which the gymnast dances, tumbles, and makes dramatic series of somersaults from one corner of the mat to the opposite. For 70 to 90 seconds, her every movement choreographed to fit the music she has chosen, the gymnast shows the judges all she can do.

At the Olympic Games and other major competitions, four to six judges at each piece of apparatus independently score the performances. The high and low scores are discarded, and the remaining scores are averaged.

Rigby performing on the uneven bars. She is shown here at the 1972 Olympics, four years after becoming a national star.

Each athlete starts with a score of 9.40; a judge may add bonus points up to a score of 10.0, or deduct tenths of points for missing components or for flaws in execution.

Gymnastics has been an Olympic sport since the first modern-times games in 1896. Until 1928, however, only men competed in Olympic gymnastics, and it was not until the 1952 Games that women were allowed to compete individually and not just for team medals.

The first great Olympic female gymnast was Agenes Keleti, who won 10 medals from 1948 to 1964. Larissa Latynina of the Soviet Union won 18 medals, including nine golds—a female Olympics record—from 1956 to 1964. (As a sign of how the age of competitors has changed over the years, when Larissa won six medals in 1964, she was 29 years old and the mother of two. Today, a gymnast past her teens is a rarity. The youth movement has been so strong that after the 1996 Games, a new rule will be imposed calling on competitors to be at least 16 years old.

Czechoslovakia's Vera Caslavska won seven Olympic gold medals, three at the 1964 Games in Tokyo and four at the 1968 Games in Mexico City. She also won silver medals both years for team and individual accomplishments.

In 1968, American fans had a new heroine to cheer. She was Cathy Rigby, a blond 15-year-old in pigtails, whose performance at the Mexico City Games changed the course of U.S. women's gymnastics.

Rigby placed only 16th in those Games, but that was the highest finish an American female gymnast had ever achieved. A fiery competitor with an engaging personality, Rigby went on to become the first American woman to win a medal in World Gymnastics competition, and she retired having won 12 international medals (eight of them gold). She was the USA Gymnastics National Women's All-Around champion in 1970 and shared the same honor two years later with Joan Moore Gnat. When ABC-TV's "Wide World of Sports" marked its 25th anniversary, Cathy was honored as one of America's Most Influential Women in Sports. Rigby later became an actress and musical comedy star.

Before Cathy Rigby endeared herself to millions of Americans, few people in the United States knew much or cared much about gymnastics. Yet other great gymnasts were in training, waiting to make names for themselves and to show the amazing feats they could perform.

2

OLGA KORBUT: A RUSSIAN REVOLUTION

If any one person can be credited with changing the course of gymnastics history, it is a little athlete in pigtails named Olga Korbut who endeared herself—and the sport—to the world at the 1972 Olympic Games in Munich, Germany.

Olga was not the best gymnast at the 1972 Games but she was certainly the most memorable. A little-known, last-minute substitute on the Soviet team, the personable 17-year-old revolutionized the sport by doing something never done before: she smiled at the audience and waved. Unlike most of her contemporaries and past gymnasts, whose expressions were as serious as ballerinas' and who performed like wind-up dolls or programmed robots, Olga

Olga Korbut shows off her amazing balance and sunny disposition.

showed her emotions and displayed a bubbly personality as she executed exciting, crowd-pleasing stunts. And when her smile turned to tears—as happened after she fell during the uneven bars finals in the all-around competition and sat weeping before the world—many of the 15,000 spectators watching her in person wept with her and millions watching on TV loved her even more.

Olga had the skills to match her charm. For example, she performed a thrilling back somersault on the balance beam, something that had never been done before. (Later, Korbut requested that the top and underside of the beam be padded, something that hadn't been necessary before she introduced her daring stunts. Today, there is thick padding under every apparatus.)

Olga was "the first gymnast to have an exciting style. Besides the difficult stunts, she gave the expression of joy to the performer," said Bela Karolyi, who is the world's most famous gymnastics coach.

Korbut took the gold medal for the beam, as well as a gold for floor exercise and a silver for the uneven bars. She also won a gold for being part of the best team, although that was due in part to the beautiful, graceful Ludmila Tourischeva, who won the all-around competition. Tourischeva went on to earn medals at three different Olympics, yet it was Korbut who reached a level of stardom never before enjoyed by a woman gymnast. As testimony to her popularity, when she did not win the uneven bars competition, the crowd's whistling in protest of the decision held up the event.

Olga stood only 4'11" and weighed 84 pounds at the Olympics. As a child, she had been bothered that she was the shortest child

in her class. But she learned to use her slight stature to her advantage. Many remember the 1972 Olympics as the saddest Games ever held—11 members of the Israeli team were kidnapped by Arab terrorists and killed in a frightening 23-hour drama. But Olga was the brightest star, "in the floor exercise, prancing like a thoroughbred going for best in show," as writer Tony Kornheiser put it.

After the Games, Olga was unquestionably the sport's number-one goodwill ambassador. At a 1975 exhibition at New York's Madison Square Garden, Korbut even overshadowed her teammate, Tourischeva, who had won more

Korbut won a gold medal for her performance on the balance beam at the 1972 Olympics.

*Russians swept the
1972 all-around medals.
Ludmila Tourischeva
(left) won the silver, Olga
Korbut (center) won
the gold, and Tamara
Lazakovitch (right) won
the bronze.*

titles than any other gymnast in history. "Olga and her Soviet teammates were so good they made bobbles look like part of the act," wrote journalist Steve Cady. "The product that emerged, as the Russians soared, twisted, and somersaulted, was one of grace and elegance and hard-to-imagine body control."

At the 1976 Games in Montreal, Canada, Korbut was a 21-year-old woman who wore heavy perfume and platform boots outside the gym, where she talked more about becoming an actress in Moscow than of continuing her quest as a gymnast. She had barely qualified as the third member of the Soviet team, though she did win a silver for the beam and shared a gold medal as a member of the victorious Soviet team.

Yet Korbut was still the beloved center of attention, still drawing squeals of admiration from her fans. Her popularity evinced shouts of "C'mon, Olga," whenever she performed, and she got more of an ovation from the spectators when she took the victory stand for her silver medal than did Nadia Comaneci, the gold-medal winner.

"For many in the crowd," wrote Neil Amdur in the *New York Times*, this was "the moment of greatest satisfaction, or perhaps sentimentality. It was the crowd's way of saying

thanks, and Olga cherished each moment, perhaps her last at this level."

If Helen of Troy's smile launched a thousands ships, Olga's infectious smile launched ten thousand new gymnastics clubs in the United States alone, as interest in the sport skyrocketed in the years following her debut. More and more youngsters took up gymnastics; more and more spectators wanted to watch the gymnasts compete. "Before Olga," said one ticket holder, "you couldn't sell a thousand tickets to a gymnastics event." Now, enthusiasts fill arenas to capacity for gymnastics events, even exhibitions.

Korbut grabbed headlines at the 1976 Olympics by performing an unusual feat of dexterity. With her chest pressed against the balance beam, she brought her legs over her head and watched her toe touch the beam in front of her. Experts debated whether this was just a contortionist's trick or a legitimate skill.

In the end, it did not matter. Olga was no longer the star; gymnastics had a newer, brighter attraction in 14-year-old Nadia Comaneci.

Korbut, however, refused to give up her crown completely. "Nadia may replace me as a gymnast," she said. "But she will never replace me as Olga Korbut."

3

NADIA COMANECI: FIRST IN PERFECTION

It was one of the most amazing Olympics performances ever.

At age 14 and weighing only 86 pounds, Nadia Comaneci (pronounced ko-man-EECH) of Romania was one of the youngest and smallest competitors at the 1976 Games. Still, she made Olympics history when she performed a breathtaking routine on the uneven bars and received the first perfect score of 10.0 ever awarded in Olympic gymnastics. Making the difficult movements look easy, Nadia executed daring, seemingly impossible stunts, which one official felt were so dangerous they should be banned. Her performance was so amazing even the scoreboard was not prepared for it. It flashed 0.00—as no one before had ever earned a 10.0, the scoreboard was not outfitted with a "1."

Nadia Comaneci, standing with her teammates, acknowledges the cheers after she scores a 10.0 at the 1976 Olympics.

The next night's program "may have been the most spectacular display of women's gymnastics ever," according to *Sports Illustrated*. Eight other gymnasts received scores of 9.90 (one of them by Olga Korbut on the uneven bars) and Ludmila Tourischeva earned a 9.95 in the floor exercise.

While the other gymnasts performed, Nadia busied herself exercising or cleaning the bars for a teammate until it was her turn. Nadia was a perfectionist and would not start a routine until everything felt right. She readied herself carefully before she took to the balance beam, and again she stuck her routine perfectly. The judges marveled, and gave her another 10.0. The crowd was awed.

Nadia then walked over to the uneven bars, where she had earned her first 10.0 the previous night, and gave an encore performance that brought the audience in the Forum in Montreal to its feet for a long ovation.

Unlike Olga Korbut, Nadia was not a naturally effervescent performer. "I never smile," she admitted, but the crowd was so insistent, she returned twice to the floor, waving to acknowledge their cheering, and even breaking into a smile when it seemed they never wanted her to leave.

With the first 10.0, Nadia made history. The next two 10.0s had the fans staggering. But before she was done, Nadia added two more 10.0 performances again on the uneven bars and beam during the all-around competition. Nadia had to settle for a 9.85 in the vault and 9.90 in the floor exercise, but that was quite enough for her to win the all-around gold medal and the highest average score ever achieved in the Olympic over-all competition.

Nadia goes head over heels as she performs a flip on the balance beam.

Nadia was the first, but not the only "perfect" gymnast at the 1976 Games. Nelli Kim of the Soviet team received a 10.0 in the vault—the first ever on that apparatus—and overtook Ludmila Tourischeva, her teammate and the defending all-around champion, for the silver medal in the all-around. The following night, Kim needed another perfect score to beat out Tourischeva for the gold in the floor exercise, and the first 10 in that event is just what she got. Then, with a 9.95, she also won the individual gold in the vault.

The relationship between the Soviet and Romanian gymnasts was cool at best. Whenever Nadia performed, Olga Korbut and her teammates, intentionally or by coincidence, often turned their backs. (Nadia also seemed to ignore Korbut's performances.) But when Comaneci was on the victory stand, Ludmila Tourischeva made what Nadia considered "a very nice gesture"—Tourischeva kissed her.

Nadia scored two more 10.0s—one on the uneven bars and one on the balance beam, for a total of seven perfect scores. Despite Tourischeva's and Kim's splendid performances, Nadia dominated the competition. She won five medals—three gold, a team silver, and a bronze for her floor exercises.

Dave Anderson of the *New York Times* wrote of Nadia, "On the uneven bars, she whirls as easily as a sparrow fluttering from limb to limb on a tree; on the balance beam, clings to it as surely as a squirrel would; on the vault, lands as softly as a sea gull on the beach. In her floor exercises, she is part go-go dancer, part ballerina, part cheerleader...."

Nadia's only difficulty during the Olympics was dealing with the press. Everyone wanted to speak with her, and she had little experience dealing with the international media. Additionally, she had everyone scrambling for Romanian interpreters, as the Russian translators the press had brought along suddenly had little to do.

In interviews immediately following her perfect performances, Nadia admitted to little more than that she was pleased with her routines and had been confident of winning. "I knew all along if I persevered and worked hard, I just might make it," she said. However, she also let it drop that she was not surprised by her 10.0s. Referring to previous competitions, she said, "I've done it 20 times now."

Nadia's training began when she was a six-year-old kindergartner in Onesti, a little town in Transylvania, Romania. Bela and Martha Karolyi wanted to develop a women's gymnastics team and had been scouting thousands of six- and seven-year-olds. The Karolyis noticed Nadia and a friend doing cartwheels better than anyone else and gave them a quick test. Nadia did a 15-meter sprint, a long jump, and a walk on the balance beam. "If they are afraid on the beam, we send them home right away," Karolyi recalled. Nadia quickly convinced the coach she had the talent and seriousness to become an excellent gymnast.

Born in 1961, Nadia was, according to Karolyi, "a kid raised in pretty hard conditions in a family without much everyday love or fun." Indeed, Romania's communist government ensured that most citizens had little money, barely enough food, and few opportunities for recreation. Karolyi invited Nadia to join his hard-working gymnastics school and she soon became the most fearless, mentally tough, and determined athlete he had. Constantly experimenting and seeking new routines, along with her teammates, she created moves between the parallel bars, performing seemingly impossible twists and spectacular dismounts. She devised a twisting, back-somersault dismount from the bars that was named after her, the "Salto Comaneci."

Critics charged some of the flips were dangerous. "Whoever is pushing them to do this is a criminal," said an international official. Despite the complaints, the Karolyis developed better and better teams and led the underdog Romanian team to upset victories over the Soviet team that had dominated the Olympics and world championships for the past 20 years.

Intensely serious and unsmiling—some people felt she was machine-like—Nadia became

*At age 14, and with
the Montreal Olympics
behind her, Nadia
returned to Romania to
help teach gymnastics
to younger children.*

Bela's most consistent gymnast after three years of training. At 13, on her way to becoming the only woman gymnast to win the European all-around championship three times in a row, the pigtailed competitor won four gold medals in the 1975 European Championships, including one for the individual all-around.

Following the 1976 Olympics, Nadia was the toast of everyone, from school kids to heads of state. She and her teammates were given high Romanian honors never before awarded to athletes.

The team, including Nadia and most of the other girls, moved to Bucharest, Romania's capital. But Bela Karolyi stayed behind and started rebuilding a team, using juniors from Onesti as a nucleus. Karolyi showed he had a magic touch as these youngsters became good enough to beat the Russians at the Friendship Cup in Cuba and performed well at the 1978 Romanian championships.

Later, a young woman appeared at Bela's door whom he hardly recognized. It was Nadia, who once had "the perfect body" for gymnastics but who had recently put on more than 40 pounds—a tremendous increase for someone who had weighed less than 90. Nadia had been completely out of gymnastics training for five months, was very depressed, and admitted she had tried to commit suicide. She pleaded for Bela to take her back into his program.

"Can you commit yourself to work like never before in your life?" he asked. "I don't know how you can do it." But Nadia wanted to be back with him and agreed to do whatever he demanded.

Karolyi agreed to take charge again of the national team and prepare it for the World Championships—only five weeks away. Then he told Nadia they'd start again. To get her back into competitive shape, he ran miles with her every day. By the time the World Championships in Strasbourg, France, started, Nadia had lost 35 pounds and was once again in "fantastic" condition.

Nadia and her unknown young teammates performed extremely well; Romania came in second place. At the European championships in Copenhagen, Denmark, Nadia won three gold medals, including one for the all-around competition.

The 1979 World Gymnastics Championships were held in Fort Worth, Texas, the first time they had been held outside of Europe. Nadia was warmly greeted in her first U.S. appearance. Her hair was shorter and she nervously bit her fingernails, but she still had consummate skill as she breezed through four compulsory events with high scores. She was leading the competition when she developed an infection in her left hand, which had to be drained at a hospital. Nadia had to withdraw. The Russian gymnasts, jubilant, expected to sweep the competition, but the remaining Romanian youngsters performed flawlessly and defeated the Soviets for the championship.

Back home, Nadia again yielded to pressure to move to Bucharest. But in June 1980, she returned to Bela, telling him she'd like to train for a shot at her second Olympics, only weeks away. He tried to discourage her, pointing out how difficult the competition would be and that unless she was "super-prepared" there was no way to win and thus it was not worth the trip. But Nadia insisted, pleading, "This is my last chance."

Karolyi relented, and although she started out in poor condition, she was in fine shape by the time the Games started in Moscow, Russia. This time, the whole world was not watching—

most Western nations boycotted the Olympics to protest the recent Soviet invasion of Afghanistan. Nadia, now an attractive 18-year-old, 5'3", 99 pounds, wearing lipstick, her hair shortened and shaped, moved, in the words of one observer, "like a well-conditioned athlete, not a neatly packaged doll."

Whatever problems she'd reportedly had—boyfriend troubles and training disagreements with her strong-willed coach—seemed behind her. Comaneci earned a perfect score on the balance beam at the beginning of the women's competition, and then 9.95s in the floor exercise, uneven bars, and vault. This left her in a tie with Natalya Shaposhnikova of the Soviet Union, who had also received one perfect score.

Two nights later, Nadia took to the beam again and gave a stellar performance. Because of a computer failure, her score wasn't posted for several minutes. When it came up 9.90, not the expected 10.0, the crowd booed and whistled in derision. The Romanian team filed a formal but futile protest.

Nadia then moved on to the uneven bars, the apparatus on which she had gained world-wide fame. In what Neil Amdur of the *New York Times* described as "the continuing drama that has made women's gymnastics the soap opera of the Summer Olympics," Nadia fell! Displaying no emotion, she quickly recovered and finished her routine. But her mark, 9.50, jeopardized her chance for the all-around title.

When Nadia approached the balance beam, her best event, she still had a shot at the gold, but she needed a score of at least 9.95. She performed superbly, but received only a 9.85, setting off one of the most controversial episodes in Olympics history. Supporters, waving Romanian flags, chanted "Na-dia, Na-dia," and she stood with hands on her hips while her angry coach argued her case passionately. The Soviets before had been accused of favoring their own, and this seemed a blatant case of prejudicial scoring. Discussions raged for half an hour, but the 9.85 mark would not be changed. Yelena Davydova of the Soviet Union won the all-around gold medal by less than a tenth of a point. Nadia tied for second.

Karolyi charged that Nadia's 9.85 score on the beam reflected "an arrangement" aimed at guaranteeing a Soviet gold medal. "It's a big injustice. Anyone who saw tonight will know Nadia was the winner."

Nadia scored another 9.85 for her beam performance on the last night of competition. That was enough to give her the total needed to win a gold medal for the apparatus, over Shaposhnikova.

Nadia's two golds and two silvers (one for the team competition) would be the last medals she would ever win. She had intended to enter the 1984 Olympics, but six weeks before the Los Angeles Games, it was announced that, at the age of 22, she was retiring from gymnastic competition in order to become a coach and a judge. Several years later, she defected from Romania and came to the United States. In 1996, she married Bart Conner, the first American male gymnast ever to win a gold medal at the Olympics.

Even after her competitive days were over, she has not been forgotten. Frank Bare, executive director of the United States Gymnastics Federation, summed up her achievements. "I think she's the best gymnast the world has ever known. She takes the basic points of a routine and does it higher and better than anyone. She's as steady as can be."

In 1980, Comaneci returned to form, winning two gold medals at the Moscow Olympics.

4

MARY LOU RETTON: ONE GREAT LEAP

Among the millions of gymnastics fans who watched Nadia Comaneci's brilliant performance at the 1976 Olympics on TV was an eight-year-old girl in Fairmont, a small mining town in West Virginia. Mary Lou Retton was enthralled by Nadia's perfect, medal-winning performance and fantasized about one day being a medal-winning Olympic gymnast herself.

Mary Lou was born on January 24, 1968, the youngest of five children. Her father had played baseball in the New York Yankees farm system and all his children were athletically talented. Mary Lou became a fearless tomboy in elementary school and could outrun any boy on the block.

"I was one of those hyper kids, always jumping up and down on the couch and break-

Mary Lou Retton exults after scoring a 10.0 on a vault in the 1984 Olympics.

ing things," recalled Mary Lou, whose mother nicknamed her "The Great Table Smasher and Lamp Toppler."

"Settle down," Mary Lou's mother used to say to her rampaging youngsters.

"Sure, Mom," they'd reply, and keep bouncing off the furniture.

When Mary Lou was four, her mother enrolled her and her sister Shari at a dance studio. Twice a week they took acrobatics, ballet, and tap-dancing lessons and learned such maneuvers as a double split. The following year, the sisters began taking twice-weekly one-hour gymnastics lessons at West Virginia University. When she was seven, Mary Lou transferred to the Aerial-port gym, where, from the outset, she demonstrated the power and explosiveness that would be her trademarks.

Mary Lou was a cheerleader, majorette, and homecoming queen, but her passion was gymnastics. As a 14-year-old high school freshman, she competed in meets throughout the world and was already the only elite gymnast in West Virginia. To maximize her talents, she realized, she'd have to leave home.

Bela Karolyi—whom she'd admired despite rumors he was a "monster" who starved his students and turned them into robots—was now running a school in Houston. He'd been impressed at a meet by Mary Lou's "hard-to-replace personality, the spirit, the guts," and he agreed to accept her as a student at Karolyi's World Gymnastics. The Rettons drove Mary Lou (accompanied by a favorite stuffed lamb) to Texas, and on New Year's Day, 1983, she bade them a tearful good-bye, moved in with a substitute family, and prepared to take a major step in her gymnastics education.

Karolyi immediately had her doing difficult, strenuous, bruising, all-out workouts. At first, "completely fatigued, mentally and physically, I was ready to go back home," Retton reported, but she stayed with it. Her perfectionist coach changed her techniques and ordered her to go on a diet.

"More bulldozer than butterfly," is how Karolyi described the 4'9", 94-pound charmer whose stocky legs and chunky, muscular body build gave her the power to run fast and leap high. Mary Lou had athletic grace to go along with her mental toughness. But her attacking style, powerful body, strut, and even her pixie hairdo were symbolic of the change from gymnasts whose looks and walks suggested models

Mary Lou Retton performs a perfect split on the balance beam.

and ballerinas. Gymnastics style now empha-sized powerful, risky, and original acrobatic stunts designed to awe spectators and judges. Typifying a new breed of gymnast, Mary Lou had power, speed, energy, and determination—and a soon-to-be-famous grin, a captivating smile that expressed her sheer joy in competing well.

Under Karolyi's tutelage, Retton's perfor-mances became more aggressive and consis-tent. Improved in all events, she built an impressive string of all-around titles. Developing more difficult skills, the dynamo with the positive attitude accidentally created what came to be known as the "Retton Salto" or "Retton Flip," in which she landed on the high bar of the uneven bars and sat there momen-tarily. Karolyi added a half-twisting movement and called it the "Retton Salto II."

Later, Mary Lou and Bela added a second full twist to the already-difficult Tsukahara vault, or "Sook" (named for Japanese Olympic gold medal-winner Mitsuo Tsukahara), creating a move no woman had previously done, and worth more than a perfect score if performed perfectly. At the American Classic, Mary Lou hopped a little on her landing but still was awarded a 10.

In New York, as an alternate for the McDonald's American Cup, a relatively new but important international competition, Mary Lou was pressed into service to replace an injured teammate. She responded well to the pressure, creating a slim lead on the first day, then lead-ing off the second with a meet record 9.95 in the vault. She won the vault and floor exercise, tied for first on bars, and won the all-around title by three-tenths of a point.

Back in Houston, practice intensified, leav-ing her so exhausted, she slept through a tornado that sliced through the house she lived in. Ironically, Mary Lou felt performing gymnastics should be such a natural reaction that "someone should be able to sneak up and drag you out at midnight, and push you on some strange floor, and you should be able to do your entire routine sound asleep in your pajamas. Without one mistake."

Entering one tournament, she was bothered by a severely painful left wrist. But having frequently endured painful and cracked bones (and even a concussion before one medal-winning competition) without complaining, she competed anyway, and had one of her best days: winning the floor, uneven bars, and vault. It turned out her wrist was broken and had to be in a cast for four weeks, causing her to miss the 1983 World Championships.

Mary Lou did, however, go to Japan in December 1983 for a major competition, the Chunichi Cup. She won the vault and became the first American to win the all-around competition. Retton began being mentioned as the biggest threat for the 1984 Olympic Games, eight months away.

Deciding to change her floor exercise in time for the 1984 McDonald's American Cup, Karolyi had a choreographer make up a new routine, a sure crowd-pleaser set to the song "Johnny, My Friend." She scored 10.0s in her floor and vault routines and won the all-around title again. (The Russians and East Germans had pulled out, saying they were worried about security for their athletes.) Ranked third at the 1984 USA National Championships, Mary Lou competed after taking a cortisone shot for a painful left foot. She scored a 10.0 and 9.90 on two vaults, winning that category, and eked out an all-around victory, a national championship.

*Mary Lou soars high
in the air on the floor
exercise on her way
to America's first
Olympic gold medal
in the all-around
competition.*

Her wrist healed in time for the Olympic trials, where she finished first. The Olympic Games were going to be held in Los Angeles, the first time the United States had hosted the Games in 52 years, and Mary Lou looked forward to competing in front of a home crowd. But in mid-June, only six weeks before the Olympics, her troublesome right knee locked and she couldn't stand up. The balloon-sized joint didn't respond to ice treatments. She did not want to have surgery, fearing it would be "all over" for her, but there was no choice. She took a private jet to Richmond, Virginia, where one of the world's best knee surgeons removed cartilage from her knee arthroscopically.

Afterwards, walking was so painful it made her cry. But Mary Lou was determined to make it to the Olympics and entered into a "nightmare" of rehabilitation back in Houston. To build her endurance, she performed strenuous exercise and in about two weeks was able to resume tumbling and landings. In July, she worked out twice a day. By Olympics time, she was ready.

Romania was the only Communist bloc nation to defy the Russians' boycott and come to Los Angeles. Mary Lou was glad the Romanians showed up as they would probably provide her greatest competition. Ecaterina Szabo was an outstanding gymnast and had been trained by Bela

Karolyi since she was five years old. By the age of seven, Szabo could do the elite compulsories; by 12, she was the European junior champion and one of strongest national team members.

The contest for the all-around gold see-sawed between Retton and Szabo, who did not perform on the same apparatus at the same time.

After Mary Lou executed what she felt was the best floor routine she'd ever done, the crowd in UCLA's Pauley Pavilion yelled, "Ten, ten, ten," but the judges awarded her a 9.95, enough to give her the lead temporarily. Szabo, smoothly welding together a variety of stunts, earned a 10.0 for her floor exercise.

Szabo then got a 10.0 on the vault, and on bars, Julianne McNamara earned the first 10.0 by any American woman in Olympics history. Mary Lou scored a 9.90.

Despite perfect marks for Julianne in her floor exercise and Mary Lou's 10.0 in the vault, the Americans couldn't catch up to the Romanians, who beat out the U.S. for the team title by a full point. Still, it was the best finish any American women's team ever had in the Olympics, and their first medal in the team competition since 1948.

Still to be determined was the best all-around woman gymnast. On the eve of the Olympics, Mary Lou had fantasized about winning. "I imagine all the moves, see myself hitting all my routines, doing everything perfectly." Visualizing the routines was one thing—now she had to go and do them.

At the all-around finals, Mary Lou had a 15-hundredths of a point lead over Szabo, who, incredibly, had landed on her face after her bars routine for a 9.30. But on the beam, Szabo, celebrated for her four backward handsprings, two more than any other competitor had attempted, earned another 10.0. And when Mary Lou, despite a Retton Flip, hopped slightly back on her landing for only a 9.85 for the uneven bars, the score was tied.

Szabo inched ahead to another 15-hundredths of a point lead and was awarded a 9.90 on the vault (in which the better score on two tries counted) despite landing with her feet spread.

Mary Lou's floor exercise was electrifying, highlighted by a high-flying double layout from corner to corner, and ending with a brilliant final pass. "No way they don't give a ten," Karolyi exclaimed. "It is the best floor routine ever done, perfection." After what seemed an eternity, the scoreboard showed the judges agreed. Mary Lou had a 10.0!

Spectators now were chanting, "U-S-A, U-S-A." But Ecaterina still led, though by a mere five-hundredths of a point.

Mary Lou arrived at her last event in the all-around competition, the vault, and the arithmetic was simple and harsh. To win the all-around title and become the first American woman to win an Olympic gold medal in gymnastics, she needed a perfect 10.0. A 9.95 would tie her with Szabo. Anything less would mean a second-place finish. All the years of painstaking, agonizing preparation had come down to an event that would be over in a matter of seconds.

Mary Lou loosened her muscles, jogged in place, rubbed her hands together. Then, when the green light signaled it was time, Mary Lou sped down the runway, rocketed off the springboard, twisted to momentary finger-contact with the apparatus and then soared into a "Sook'" layout in inimitable Retton fashion, before sticking her landing so solidly she shook the arena. Jubilantly, she threw up her arms in victory, waved a fist, clapped her hands, tossed back her head, confident she'd nailed the score she needed. The crowd leaped to its feet to give her a standing ovation for what *Sports Illustrated* would call "A Vault Without Fault" and what Don Peters, coach of the U.S. women's Olympic gymnastic team, called "the best vault I've ever seen."

"I knew by my takeoff that I had it," Mary Lou said afterward. "I knew by my vault that I had it. I knew it when I was in the air! Nobody thought it could be done. But you know what? I went and did it."

The scoreboard confirmed what everyone already knew: She had earned a 10.0, and had become the first American, male or female, to win the all-around title in Olympic gymnastics. Indeed, she was the first American woman ever to win gold in any Olympics gymnastics category.

Vaulters are permitted to do their routines twice and use the higher of the two scores. Mary Lou was sure of her 10, and there was no reason to do the vault again. Yet she chose to do an encore. And, believe it or not, she gave another perfect performance, a carbon copy of the first, except perhaps that she maybe stuck the landing even more firmly.

The only gymnast to qualify for all four event finals, Mary Lou came away with the all-around gold, silvers for team and in the vault behind Szabo, bronzes on the uneven bars and floor, and fourth place on beam. "Not bad," she said. "I've got at least one of each color." Her five medals were the most won by any athlete at the 1984 Olympics.

Before Mary Lou retired, she achieved one more memorable mark. In March 1985, in Indi-

After the Olympics, Mary Lou Retton and other 1984 Olympic medalists marched in a parade at Disney World.

anapolis, Mary Lou became the first female gymnast to win three consecutive McDonald's American Cup all-around championships. Said Karolyi: "I guarantee no gymnast in the world could have done what Mary Lou has. Nadia was a great champion, but Mary Lou is bigger. That strong a personality is fantastic, unbelievable." In 25 years of teaching gymnastics, he said, "I had many world and Olympic champions, but I never had somebody more positive and dedicated than this little girl."

Mary Lou's winning style and smile made her a role model for millions of Americans. She was honored at parades, from Fairmont to New York City, and sought out by corporations as their spokesperson or motivational speaker, often promoting the benefits of proper nutrition and regular exercise. She got mail from all over and, easily recognized by her smile, was besieged by autograph-seekers. The first woman athlete to have her image appear on Wheaties boxes, Mary Lou appeared on TV shows and in the Macy's Thanksgiving Day Parade, and was a presenter at the Emmy Awards and TV commentator for the 1988 Olympics.

In December 1984, she was named "Sportswoman of the Year" by *Sports Illustrated* (whose Bob Ottum had written, "At last, the average-size people of America have a heroine they can look down on") and the same year she was named Associated Press Amateur Athlete of the Year. Her smile was featured on scores of covers of major magazines.

In a 1993 Associated Press national survey, Mary Lou was voted "Most Popular Athlete in America." In 1994, the U.S. Olympic Committee established the annual Mary Lou Retton Award for athletic excellence, and Hillary Clinton presented her with the Flo Hyman Award in recognition of her spirit, dignity and commitment to excellence.

Mary Lou has appeared in two movies, *Scrooged* and *Naked Gun 33 1/3*, and on numerous TV shows, including soap operas and "Baywatch."

After taking a correspondence course for her high school diploma she majored in communications at the University of Texas. She married Shannon Kelley in 1990 and gave birth to a daughter, Shayla Rae, on April 12, 1995. And every so often she thinks about her moments on the victory stand. "I had an experience that is indescribable," she says. "The gold medal around my neck, my hand over my heart, the American flag raising, the national anthem—it's something I will never forget."

5

SHANNON MILLER: MOST DECORATED AMERICAN

For Shannon Miller, the leap to stardom began with a trampoline her parents bought her for Christmas when she was five years old. Soon her imaginative jumping prompted her parents to enroll her in a local gymnastics program.

When her club traveled to Russia for a clinic in 1986, Shannon saw some of the world's best gymnasts in action. She cried out of frustration that she could not duplicate the difficult maneuvers the older athletes were doing. But Steve Nunno, former assistant to Bela Karolyi, recognized her potential and was impressed by the determined way she kept trying to do the tricks. "I thought, now there's a girl for me," said Nunno, who became Shannon's coach at her Oklahoma City club. Within two years,

Shannon Miller does a flip on the balance beam en route to winning a silver medal at the 1992 Olympics.

Miller was performing at the national level; two years later, she was considered world class.

As hard as she worked at perfecting her gymnastic skills—adhering to an arduous 35-hour weekly training schedule that started before school and extended into the evenings and weekends—she managed to excel in scholastics as well as athletics. At Edmond North Mid-High School, in Edmond, Oklahoma, Shannon was a straight-A student. As a freshman at Oklahoma University, she maintained a 4.0 grade point average, which, like a 10.0 in gymnastics, is as good as it gets.

Born in Rolla, Missouri, on March 10, 1977, Shannon grew up in Edmond, where, unlike some star gymnasts who left their families to train elsewhere, she lived with her parents, Ron, a physics professor, and Claudia, a bank executive. As a Junior gymnast, the tiny competitor—Shannon was then only 4'7" and weighed just 70 pounds—made strong showings in national and international competitions in 1988 and 1989. In 1991, she got perfect scores on balance beam in two competitions in Switzerland—at one of those, winning gold in the all-around and on every apparatus.

At the World Gymnastics Championships in Indianapolis in 1991, Shannon became the first American woman to qualify for the finals in all four events, and tied for second on the uneven bars. In the team competition, she was the top scorer for the U.S., helping the American women gymnasts win a silver medal, its first medal of any kind in a world championship.

In March 1992, two months before the nationals, Shannon dislocated her left elbow and needed surgery and a microscrew to fix it. But only one day later, the determined youngster was back in training.

Miller won an Olympic bronze medal in 1992 for this performance on the uneven bars.

At the 1992 nationals, Miller led on the vault, balance beam, and floor exercise in the compulsories (in which every athlete must perform the same routines on every apparatus). But she withdrew from the more difficult, optional routine portion of the competition because she hadn't had enough practice. Shannon's withdrawal meant that her chance to make the Olympic team would hinge entirely on her scores at the forthcoming Olympic trials in Baltimore.

Performing at her best when it counted the most, Shannon won the all-around at the Olympic trials. She loomed as the American women's best hope for Olympic gold.

Said Coach Nunno: "It's no longer a question if Shannon is going to be on the Olympic team. Now the question is how many medals she'll win in Barcelona."

At the 1992 Olympics in Spain, Shannon performed to expectations. Matching Mary Lou

Retton's accomplishment, she won five medals (three of them in one night). Her second-place silver in the all-around was the highest finish by an American gymnast at a non-boycotted Olympics since the Soviets began participating in 1952. She was the only gymnast to compete in all four individual events, and the only American to win an individual medal.

Shannon received the 1992 Sports Headliner of the Year Award for Oklahoma and that year became the first female to win the Steve Reeves Fitness Award presented by the Downtown Athletic Club.

In 1993, a year when she nearly gave up gymnastics, she won four gold medals (all-around, vault, uneven bars, and floor exercises) at the McDonald's American Cup in Orlando, Florida, and three gold medals (all-around, uneven bars, and floor exercise) at the World Gymnastics Championships in Birmingham, England. At the 1993 Coca-Cola National Championships in Salt Lake City, she took gold for all-around, uneven bars, and floor exercise; silver in the vault; and bronze in the balance beam.

The following year, at the World Gymnastics Championships in Brisbane, Australia, she became the only American woman in history to win consecutive World Championship all-around titles, and also won gold for balance beam. Coach Nunno had built a rehab center at his gym, and bought a 60-foot trampoline ramp to ease the pounding Miller's knees, ankles, and back took during tumbling maneuvers. "Without that," he commented, "she wouldn't have won the world championship this year. She might not have competed."

Despite her successes, changes were ocurring physically for Miller. By the end of 1994, when she won the Dial Award as the nation's top female high school student-athlete, Shannon had grown 4 inches and gained 20 pounds. She now stood 4'11" and weighed 90 pounds. "This," wrote Jere Longman in the *New York Times*, "has shifted her center of gravity and changed her performance from pipsqueak with a rubber-band body to young woman of confidence, power and sophistication."

Some adjustments had to be made. For instance, to make up for diminished speed on twists and spins, her coach had Shannon emphasize power in vaulting and tumbling. Needing more rest than she did early in her career, Shannon left competition part-way at the 1994 Team World Championships in Dortmund, Germany.

Shannon was no longer one of what Longman characterized as the "athletic munchkins" whose acrobatic stunts, since 1976 and Nadia Comaneci, he said, had come to be preferred by judges, officials, and coaches over "maturity, grace and elegance." Now 17, Miller was determined to prove that "you don't have to be a young kid to perform difficult routines." Accordingly, she worked on developing innovative, difficult routines with elements not previously attempted, and they seemed to be doing the trick.

In the 1995 Pan American Games in Mar Del Plata, Argentina, Shannon won the all-around (with a score of 38.587 to Amanda Borden's 38.575), floor exercises, and took second in the vault.

Then, at the 1995 Coca-Cola National Championships in New Orleans, Shannon led after the compulsories but fell in her first optional routine on the balance beam. But the

*Shannon Miller smiles
as her coach, Steve
Nunno, signifies she is
number one after she won
the gold medal for overall
performance at the 1994
World Gymnastic
Championships.*

skillful veteran kept her cool; she climbed back up and nailed a twisting double-back dismount. Shannon finished second in the all-around to Dominique Moceanu by only two-tenths of a point and took the gold in the vault.

Shannon's self-assurance seemed to have grown. "She's always been known as shy, but now she comes in the gym and takes over," said Peggy Liddick, Miller's coach on the balance beam and choreographer of her floor routine. "Her inhibitions have subsided."

The 1995 World Championships at Sabae, Japan, looked promising for Miller, who had won the individual all-around in that competition the last two years. But, troubled by a sore ankle and a slip on the uneven bars, she managed only a 12th-place finish in the all-around; tied for fourth on the beam, and finished seventh on the uneven bars. However, Shannon remained confident. She'd rebounded from disappointment before.

Three times she was voted the USOC SportsWoman of the Month and was a finalist for the Zaharias Award in 1992, 1993, and 1994. At the 1994 Goodwill Games, along with Russia's Dina Kochetkova, Miller was honored as the most popular gymnast, and was the 1994 inaugural recipient of the Henry P. Iba Citizen Athlete Award.

Nicknamed the "Mag 7" (short for the Magnificent 7), Shannon's teammates at the 1996 Olympics in Atlanta, Georgia, were Dominique Moceanu, Dominique Dawes, Kerri Strug (more about these gymnasts appears in the next chapter), along with Amanda Borden, Amy Chow, and Jaycee Phelps. Under the guidance of Coach Martha Karolyi (husband Bela stood on the sidelines, shouting encouragement), Shannon led her team to the first gold medal ever won by an American women's team. In the team competition, her gutsy performance on the balance beam steadied her team after two previous American women faltered. Miller was the picture of control at all events.

Shannon did falter after the team competition. She was in second place after two events of the all-around competition, but a low mark in the floor exercises dropped her out of the running for a medal. She did cap off her Olympics with a gold medal on the balance beam.

Shannon has already won more medals at the Olympics (7) and World Championships (9) than any other U.S. gymnast in history, male or female. But she's not content to retire on her laurels. Years ago, she said she'd stay with gymnastics "until I get bored, or until I stop learning new things."

Only time will tell where Miller's career takes her next.

6

TODAY'S STARS

D OMINIQUE MOCEANU

Dominique Moceanu's gymnastics talent can probably be attributed to good genes. Both her parents, Dumitru and Camelia, who settled in California in 1980, were gymnasts in their native Romania. Her mother was a Level-10 gymnast there, and her father, a member of the Romanian Junior National Team.

Before Dominique was born, her father was determined that she'd become a gymnast or other type of athlete. "I wanted her to have the discipline." When Dominique was 3, he tested her strength by seeing how long she could hang from a clothesline. Talk about tenacity: the line broke before she let go.

Her parent's aptitude for gymnastics has certainly been passed along dramatically, with Dominique establishing a series of remarkable

Svetlana Boginskaya helped the Russian team win numerous medals at the 1992 Olympics.

firsts as the "youngest" to achieve some significant milestones in gymnastics.

Born September 30, 1981, in Hollywood, California, she was only 10 when she qualified for the U.S. Junior National Team, the youngest athlete ever to make the team. Dominique then made the leap from being Junior National Champion in 1994 to Senior National Champion the following year when she was still 13, to become the youngest in history to win that title.

The cherub with the dazzling smile won her first international all-around title at the 1995 Visa Challenge (where she also won gold for team and floor exercise; silver for uneven bars, and bronze for vault and balance beam). In 1995, she was all-around champion at the World Team Trials in Austin, Texas; at the Coca-Cola National Championships in New Orleans that year, with no score lower than 9.725, she won gold for all-around (by two-tenths of a point over Shannon Miller), plus silver for floor exercise and bronze for vault. At the 1995 World Championships in Sabae, Japan, Dominique tied for second on the balance beam, and contributed to a third-place team finish.

Moceanu's gifted performance at the 1996 Olympics was overshadowed by her consecutive poor vaults as the U.S. was hoping to wrap up the team gold. This led to a heroic vault by Kerry Strug that clinched the victory. When Strug was unable to enter the all-around competition, Moceanu took her place but won no further medals. Still, of all the "Mag 7" members, she is the most likely to be back in the 2000 Olympics.

Bela Karolyi, with his wife, Martha, has been coaching Dominique since 1990 (after having turned her down previously because she was too young). The Moceanus, who had lived in Illinois and Florida after California, moved to Houston, Texas, so Dominique could train at Karolyi's. (Her kid sister trains there, too.)

Karolyi, who compares Dominique's performance enjoyment to Mary Lou Retton's, considers Moceanu's physical capabilities great and her 4'5", 70-pound body well-proportioned and ideal for gymnastics. "But I think the most positive thing about Dominique is her personality. She's like a little bird, always a smile on her face. That's what is needed in the sport."

SVETLANA BOGINSKAYA

In a sport dominated by tiny teenagers, gymnast Svetlana Boginskaya of Belarus in the former Soviet Union stands out—in more ways than one.

A long-legged, 5'4" beauty who is now 23, the mature-looking athlete towers above many if not most of her rivals, projecting what one writer called "that magical presence that captivates audiences."

Svetlana has won five Olympic medals (three gold) and nine World Championship medals, and is riding the wave of a surprisingly successful comeback. Because few world-class women gymnasts compete beyond their mid- or late teens, no one expected Svetlana to return to competition after she retired following the 1992 Olympics. But the gymnast, who is known variously as "Queen of Perfection," "Belarussian Swan," and "The Goddess of Gymnastics" has roared back into contention.

At the McDonald's American Cup in March 1996, skillfully executing routines that are difficult for a gymnast of her size, she finished second to American Kerri Strug with a dazzling performance. Later that month, demonstrating a wide variety of skills combined with excellent choreography, she helped her Belarussian team to a gold medal at McDonald's Three-on-Three competition among teams comprised of a male and female gymnast and a rhythmic gymnast.

"A great athlete, a joy to see on the floor," are the words of Bela Karolyi, who is now Svetlana's coach. Ironically, for much of his career Karolyi, a pioneer of "tiny tot" gymnasts rather than more mature competitors, was an arch rival of Soviet women gymnasts, including Svetlana, and had offered some unflattering comments about her in the past. But Boginskaya and American gymnast Kim Zmeskal, who had edged her out for the gold at the 1991 World Championships, independently convinced Karolyi to come out of retirement to coach them.

Today, Bela cheers Svetlana's triumphant return to the sport at 23, calling her "the surprise of the gymnastics community." Her experience and maturity is "what this sport really needed at this time."

Svetlana started in gymnastics when she was seven, pushed into the sport by her father, a builder, and mother, a housewife, from Minsk in Belarus. "It was boring for me at home." she told an interviewer. "So in the first years of school, when a lady coach came and asked who wanted to go into gymnastics, I agreed. I wasn't much of a gymnastic fan then, but my parents said they'd better send me to some sports group because I wasn't obedient at home and didn't listen to them." Three years later, she began attending training camp, away from her parents, at first for ten days a year and then for longer and longer periods. For the girl who would become one of the most decorated gymnasts of her time, life was almost exclusively gymnastics.

Coming into the 1988 Olympics in Seoul, Korea, Boginskaya and other members of the Soviet Union team were told they were not only performing for themselves but representing "the image of the Soviet Union." The team took first place, and Svetlana also won gold in the vault and a bronze in the all-around.

Described by a *New York Times* writer as "a grim-faced athlete who seldom smiles or reveals any sort of emotion while performing," Svetlana won silver behind Zmeskal at the 1991 World Championships. Some felt American judges had tilted the scoring in favor of their own. Reminded the next year of her second-place finish, she cried for a moment, then said: "Well, it's all in the past. Of course, I want to be the best. I've always been that way."

Before the 1992 Olympic Games, supposedly her last, Svetlana acknowledged feeling "some uncertainty." Then 19, she said, "It becomes harder for me to train the same way as before. When I was younger, I did many of the elements easier than now and sometimes I make errors. And, of course, when I was younger, we studied new aspects all the time. Now it's more routine work for me. It's repetition and repetition, which is, of course, less interesting."

To minimize nervousness, she tried to think about the forthcoming Barcelona Games not as the Olympics but as "just another competition." She competed as a member of the Unified Team, made up of gymnasts from four former Soviet republics, teammates for the last time. This team took first place, the Soviets' tenth consecutive victory in the Summer Games, which it had attended since 1952.

Kim Zmeskal was one of America's brightest hopes for medals at the 1992 Olympics.

In the optional round, the routines of Svetlana and other Soviet teammates were described as "typically bold, inventive, and esthetically pleasing." One of three of her team's gymnasts (the maximum) who advanced to the all-around competition, Svetlana failed to win an individual medal, finishing fifth in the all-around and beam, and fourth in the vault.

After the Games, Svetlana "retired," but at 21 came to Houston "so happy" to be coached by Karolyi. If not for residency requirements, she'd probably perform for the U.S. team.

"In 1988," she told NBC Sports, "I was too little to realize it was the Olympics. It was a big deal for me. In 1992, it was too much pressure."

Svetlana performed well at the 1996 Olympics but did not win any medals.

KIM ZMESKAL

In a pressure-cooker sport like competitive gymnastics, being on top isn't always the best place to be. At least it wasn't for Kim Zmeskal, whose fortunes have swung like a gymnast on the uneven bars.

Coming into the 1992 Olympics, the young American was considered the world's top female gymnast. Then a combination of injury and missteps, compounded by pressure to succeed, broke her confidence and drove her into early retirement. She came out of retirement in 1994, inspired by a champion Olympic ice skater making a comeback.

"This one's a tiger," Bela Karolyi had said with admiration, describing Kim, then a 4'7", 80-pound 15-year-old, who won the all-around title at the 1991 World Championships in Indianapolis. With that victory, sparked by the competition's only 10 (in vault in team competition), Zmeskal broke the Soviet Union's long-time gold-medal monopoly and became the first American gymnast, male or female, to win an all-around title in the world championships.

To win the gold, Kim—named "1991 SportsWoman of the Year" by the U.S. Olympic Committee—beat out Svetlana Boginskaya of Belarussia, the defending world champion who had won four medals at the 1988 Olympics in Seoul, Korea. This was the most spectacular world championships ever, declared Karolyi, "and overall they show what the Americans can do right now."

There was a new format at the following year's World Championships: individual event titles, but none for team or all-around. Zmeskal won two golds—one in floor exercise and then outscoring Boginskaya on balance beam. Kim was the only competitor to win more than one event. And, by performing routines rated at higher levels of difficulty than those of her competitors, Kim won a gold medal for all-around at McDonald's American Cup in Orlando, Florida, and her third consecutive all-around national title at the U.S. Gymnastic Championships, held in Columbus, Ohio. There, she was first in the floor exercise and tied for gold on the beam; she was second in bars and vault. (She got a 10 in the vault prelims, one of eight perfect scores has achieved in her career.)

For Kim, chosen "1992 Athlete of the Year" by her national teammates, everything was golden. But it was too good to last. First, that June in Baltimore, Kim, the favorite, finished second to Shannon Miller at the Olympic trials. "Placing is not so important as correcting mistakes," Zmeskal said. "I made some mistakes."

When the scene shifted to Barcelona and the 1992 Summer Olympic Games, Kim fell from grace, literally. On her first apparatus, the balance beam, she rotated backwards with her legs split. When her right foot failed to land, she lost her balance and had to jump off. "I was really excited to get this started," she explained. "I had a lot of energy. But the beam is not the best event to have too much energy."

The mishap put her in 32nd place, but she improved her position with a 9.912 score on the beam and a 9.95 on the vault. Her woes were not over, however. On the last tumbling maneuver of her floor exercise, she stepped out of bounds, for an automatic one-tenth point deduction. "I did not have the night of my life," she said. You have one night to hit. If you're on, you're on.... But even when I did hit, my scores were not very high. I was lucky to get as much as I did."

Hanging tough, she climbed back to a high-enough position to qualify as the third American (three being the limit for each team) for the all-around, in which she finished tenth. "I have never been under such pressure. But it was a pretty strong effort," said Kim, who won a bronze medal as a member of the third-place U.S. team but finished eighth in the vault and sixth in the floor exercise.

It was a very disappointing showing. According to her coach, Karolyi, Zmeskal "had turned from the most confident person I ever had into a timid individual, a broken bird."

"Her destructive period started long before this," said Karolyi at a news conference. "She was called the best in the world and it created an absurd situation—up and down. It ground her little heart to pieces and pieces.... If I could

blame anybody, it would be the people who created the monster...the people and media that put
her on the pedestal and the judges who tore her
apart."

Dejected, Kim went back to high school,
where, she said, according to Jere Longman,
writing in the *New York Times*, "I didn't feel the
need to make a spectacle of myself." At
Westfield High School, from which she graduat-
ed in 1994, Kim was a member of the National
Honor Society.

Her retirement lasted only until 1994. The
Houston-born competitor, who'd trained at
Karolyi's since she started gymnastics at the
age of six, had watched the 1994 Winter
Olympics, in which Brian Boitano was making
a comeback in figure skating, and something
clicked.

"I felt like he was talking to me. He said he
missed the sport, and he still wanted to enjoy it
while he could. There was nothing to prove. He
was doing it because that's what he wanted
to do."

In May 1994, Kim decided to come out of
retirement and train in hopes of participating in
the 1996 Olympics. Her old injuries flared up,
however, and she had to root for her old teammates from the sidelines.

DOMINIQUE DAWES

Her coach, Kelli Hill, and her "Hill's Angels"
teammates call her "Awesome Dawesome," and
indeed Dominique Dawes is a powerful, dynam-
ic gymnast who has given truly awe-inspiring
performances. A prime example: her spectacular sweep of the 1994 Coca-Cola National
Championships in Nashville, Tennessee, where
she won gold in the all-around and all four

apparatus events. Dawes was the first to accomplish that feat in 26 years.

Dominique, born in Silver Spring, Maryland, on November 20, 1976, has been in gymnastics since 1983. A strong tumbler, she earned her first '10' in international competition in 1992 with her floor exercise in the USA versus Japan dual competition.

Dawes made the 1992 U.S. Olympic team, despite falling off the beam in her compulsory round during a pre-Olympics competition. At the 1992 Games in Barcelona, she shared in the team bronze medal for its third-place finish.

Steadily improving, at the 1993 Coca-Cola Nationals in Salt Lake City, Dawes won gold medals in the vault and beam, silver in the all-around and floor exercise, and bronze in the uneven bars. At the World Gymnastics Championships in Birmingham, Great Britain, that year, she earned silver medals in the uneven bars and balance beam, and finished fourth in the all-around.

Dawes took first-place in the all-around, vault, beam, and floor exercise at the 1994 McDonald's American Cup in Orlando, Florida, and first place in the NationsBank World Team Trials in Richmond, but did not fare as well at the 1994 World Gymnastics Championships in Brisbane, Australia, finishing fifth in the all-around. She did, however, share in team silver at the 1994 Team World Championships in Dortmund, Germany, her fourth competition as a World Championship team member. An injury kept her out of the 1995 World Championships.

She's demonstrated the ability to bounce back from adversity, no more dramatically than at the 1995 Coca-Cola National Championships in New Orleans, which she entered as reigning champion, having dominated the event a year earlier. But at the 1995 competition, Dominique was one of several veteran gymnasts to fall or stumble at critical moments, and she finished in fourth place in the all-around. Yet she rallied to win the gold in two events — the uneven bars and floor exercises — and bronze on the beam. (She was fourth in the vault.)

Dominique, a resident of Gaithersburg, Maryland, who trains at Hill's Gymnastics, enjoys reading books, dancing, and acting. She enrolled in the fall of 1995 as a freshman at the University of Maryland after having been an honor roll student in high school and prom queen at her senior prom.

Domique was a big contributor to the gold-medal performance for the U.S. women's team at the 1996 Olympics. After two events in the all-around, she was in first place, but on a tumbling run on the floor apparatus, she came down heavily and stepped out of bounds. The big deduction left her out of the medal picture. However, she performed brilliantly on the floor exercises in the individual competition, winning a bronze medal.

KERRI STRUG

Americans will long remember the vault Kerri Strug performed that clinched the U.S. team's gold medal at the 1996 Olympics. After Dominique Moceanu scored poorly on two vaults, falling both times, Strug needed only one good vault to give the Americans some breathing room.

Strug fell on her first vault, severely hurting her already injured ankle in the process. But with her coaches urging her on, she vaulted again, this time nailing her landing, even

Dominique Dawes holds a handstand at the 1996 World Gymnastic Championships, where she won a bronze medal.

though she fell to the ground moments after, her face contorted in pain. The image of Bela Karolyi scooping her up after her fall and Strug receiving her medal with her leg in a cast are two of the most indelible to come out of the 1996 Olympics.

Strug has long been familiar with injuries. Indeed, her appearance in Atlanta marked a comeback for her, as some thought her days as a championship gymnast were already behind her. Changes in coaches and gyms had done little to restore the confidence of someone who had started out so brilliantly.

At the 1992 Games in Barcelona, Strug, then 14, was the youngest member of the U.S. Olympic team. She won a bronze medal when the U.S. team took third place at the Olympics. Kerri has done well in other major competitions, including first on the balance beam and second in the all-around at the 1993 McDonald's American Cup at Orlando, Florida.

But no matter how well she performed, she felt overshadowed by such stars as Kim Zmeskal, Shannon Miller, and Dominique Moceanu, and it was frustrating. Talented but timid, she was beset by nervousness and found her confidence wanting.

Strug kept changing from one coach to another, in different parts of the United States, for a while training in Oklahoma with Shannon Miller. Between changes in coaches and gyms, a fall and torn stomach muscle and other injuries further contributed to her discouragement.

But the world-class athlete from Tucson, Arizona, rebounded. Steadily improving, she helped lead the U.S. women to the silver medal at the Team World Championships in Dortmund, Germany, in 1994.

In March 1996, at the McDonald's American Cup in Fort Worth, Texas, with Miller and Dominique Moceanu sidelined by injuries, Kerri capitalized on her opportunities and won the gold. She edged out two gymnasts who'd been members of the Unified Team at the 1992 Olympics, Svetlana Boginskaya of Belarus, who finished second at the American Cup, and Oksana Chusotivina of Uzbekistan, who came in third. With strong routines and new-found confidence, Kerri finally won the American Cup. She was, she admitted, "a little bit nervous," but had performed so many times she knew she could do it.

After her memorable Olympic vault in 1996, Strug qualified for the all-around competition. However, she had to cede her place to Dominique Moceanu when her ankle did not heal quickly enough. It did not matter. She came out of the Olympics as the newest star gymnast, the latest in the line started by Olga and Nadia, a heroine of the sport.

CHRONOLOGY

1964   Larissa Latynina of the Soviet Union wins six medals in her third
        Olympic appearance. At age 29 and the mother of two, she won 18
        medals, including nine golds — more than any other gymnast in
        history.

1968   Vera Caslavska of Czechoslovakia wins four gold medals at the
        Olympics; she had previously won three golds at the 1964
        Olympics. Cathy Rigby finishes 16th, the highest finish for any
        American gymnast.

1972   Olga Korbut of the Soviet Union becomes the first "star" gymnast
        with a popular following.

1976   Nadia Comaneci becomes the first gymnast to score a 10.0 in
        Olympic history. She goes on to score six other 10.0s and walks
        away with the all-around title.

1980   Nadia Comaneci comes out of exile to win two golds and two silvers
        at the Moscow Olympics—which the U.S. and many non-
        Communist countries boycott.

1984   Mary Lou Retton scores a dramatic 10.0 and wins America's first
        Olympic gold medal in gymnastics. She also wins a gold in the all-
        around competition in an Olympics boycotted by many Communist
        countries.

1992   Shannon Miller wins five medals at the Barcelona Olympics.

1996   The U.S. team wins its first gold medal at the Atlanta Olympics
        after a heroic vault by Kerri Strug.

SUGGESTIONS FOR FURTHER READING

Arnold, Caroline. *The Olympic Summer Games.* New York: Franklin Watts, 1991.

Aykroyd, Peter. *Modern Gymnastics.* New York: Arco, 1985.

Berke, Art. *Gymnastics.* New York: Franklin Watts, 1988.

Murdock, Tony, and Nik Stuart. *Gymnastics: A Practical Guide for Beginners.* New York: Franklin Watts, 1989.

Retton, Mary Lou and Bela Karolyi with John Powers. *Mary Lou: Creating an Olympic Champion.* New York: McGraw-Hill, 1986.

Silverman, Herma. *Mary Lou Retton and the New Gymnasts.* New York: Franklin Watts, 1985.

Slear, Tom. *Where Imagination Becomes Reality.* Minneapolis: Professional Sports Publications, 1994.

ABOUT THE AUTHOR

JOEL H. COHEN is the author of 30 published books, most of them for younger readers. A graduate of Wagner College and the Columbia University Graduate School of Journalism, he has written for numerous magazines, including *TV Guide* and *Sports Illustrated for Kids.* He and his wife have four children and live in Staten Island, New York.

INDEX

Amdur, Neil, 17, 26
Anderson, Dave, 22
Bare, Frank, 27
Boginskaya, Svetlana, 49,
  51-54, 55, 61
Boitano, Brian, 57
Borden, Amanda, 46
Cady, Steve, 16
Caslavska, Vera, 10
Chow, Amy, 46
Chusotivina, Oksana, 61
Clinton, Hillary, 38
Comaneci, Nadia, 17, 19-27,
  29, 37, 46
Conner, Bart, 27
Davydova, Yelena, 27
Dawes, Dominique, 46, 57-59
Gnat, Joan Moore, 11
Hill, Kelli, 57

Karolyi, Bela, 14, 22-25, 27,
  30-32, 34, 36, 37, 42, 50,
  51-52, 54, 57
Karolyi, Martha, 22-23, 50
Keleti, Agenes, 10
Kelly, Shannon, 39
Kelly, Shayla Rae, 39
Kim, Nelli, 20-21
Korbut, Olga, 13-17, 20, 21
Kornheiser, Tony, 15
Latynina, Larissa, 10
Liddick, Peggy, 47
Longman, Jere, 45
McNamara, Julianne, 35
Miller, Claudia, 43
Miller, Ron, 43
Miller, Shannon, 41-47, 50,
  56, 60
Moceanu, Camelia, 49, 50

Moceanu, Dominique, 46, 49-
  51, 60, 61
Moceanu, Dumitru, 49, 50
Nunno, Steve, 42, 44, 45, 47
Ottum, Bob, 38
Peters, Don, 37
Phelps, Jaycee, 46
Retton, Mary Lou, 29-39, 44
Retton, Shari, 30
Rigby, Cathy, 7, 9, 10-11
Shaposhnikova, Natalya, 26,
  27
Strug, Kerri, 46, 50, 59-61
Szabo, Ecaterina, 34-36, 37
Tourischeva, Ludmila, 14, 15,
  16, 20-22
Tsukahara, Mitsuo, 32
Zmeskal, Kim, 52, 53,
  54-57, 60

PICTURE CREDITS

AP/Wide World: pp. 2, 6, 9, 12, 15, 21, 27, 28, 31, 34, 37, 46; UPI/Bettmann: p. 16 ; Corbis: pp. 18, 24, 40, 43 48, 58; Archive Photos: p. 51.